Dessert
Bouquets

O8-CYV-219

Create Your Own Gifts & Centerpieces

Delicious Designs

Printed in China

Published By:

CQ Products

507 Industrial Street
Waverly, IA 50677

ISBN-13: 978-1-56383-401-1
ISBN-10: 1-56383-401-4
Item #3628

Table of Contents

Getting Started

Add the finishing touch to a special meal when you make dessert that serves double-duty as an edible centerpiece or bouquet. Every meal deserves dessert, but a dessert bouquet shows guests you care. These bouquets also make a striking and greatly appreciated gift. Our photos and step-by-step instructions make it easy to turn ordinary treats into extraordinary displays. So, why just make dessert? Make it extra special with a dessert bouquet!

Food Safety

Before you begin any food project, be sure to thoroughly clean your hands, containers, utensils and work surface. Use knives properly with a cutting board below and practice general kitchen safety when using sharp utensils.

Choose the freshest fruits and food items available to help make your bouquet as special as the event for which it's being prepared. Wash fresh fruits gently but thoroughly to remove dirt and bacteria and be sure to pat dry with paper towels before using.

Bouquets made from fresh fruit should be kept cool and served shortly after assembly or stored for a short time, loosely covered, in the refrigerator.

Some bouquets, such as those made from chocolate, need to be kept cool to prevent melting. Store them in a cool location out of direct sunlight.

Gather Some General Supplies

All of these supplies can be found easily in any grocery store, kitchen shop and the craft or baking section of most discount stores. However, if you have trouble locating an item, be sure to ask at the store or go to the manufacturer's website for assistance. Keep in mind that some items are seasonal and may be available only at certain times of the year.

- *Food-safe containers*
- *Styrofoam ("foam")*
- *Knife for trimming foam*
- *Pruning shears*
- *Tape*
- *Waxed paper*
- *Aluminum foil*
- *Plastic wrap*
- *Parchment paper*
- *Cutting board*
- *Sharp knives*
- *Cookie cutters (metal and plastic)*
- *Tissue paper*
- *Nonstick cooking spray*
- *Heavy-duty zippered plastic bags*
- *Pastry bags fitted with decorative tips*
- *White lollipop sticks*
- *White cookie sticks*
- *Wooden or bamboo skewers*
- *Toothpicks*
- *Food coloring (Gel or paste coloring is recommended for the best color and consistency.)*
- *Ribbons and other embellishments*

Prepare the Base

Choosing a container for your dessert bouquet is an important consideration. It should be attractive, sturdy and appropriately sized for your bouquet. Keep in mind that a container can sometimes be painted or covered in paper, if needed, to fit the theme and color of your bouquet.

In some bouquets, a food product may be used inside the container for the base. This might include an item that can be eaten along with the bouquet, such as a pan of bars or a pineapple, or it might be a product that will not be consumed, such as a head of lettuce.

Sometimes, directions call for a non-edible base made from Styrofoam. In that case, use a piece of foam that most closely matches your container's size and shape. To trim foam to fit, simply press the container's opening against the foam to make an outline. Use a knife to cut about ½″ inside the outline, angling cuts as needed so foam fits into container. Keep the foam about 1″ below the top of the container, unless directed otherwise.

Since foam can be dangerous if ingested, wrap it in aluminum foil, plastic wrap or waxed paper to prevent contact with food. The foil can be disguised by arranging food over the top or by simply covering it with shredded paper or tissue paper.

Food Placement

A great way to display food in a bouquet is to skewer food items on plain or frill toothpicks, bamboo or wooden cocktail picks, plastic drink stirrers and white lollipop or cookie sticks. Simple bamboo skewers, 10″ to 12″ long, are inexpensive, versatile and easy to find. Quite often, longer skewers will need to be trimmed. To trim, simply cut to length with a clean, sanitary pruning shears.

Sometimes foods will slip down a skewer after assembly. To prevent this, simply place a "stopper", such as a raisin, dried cranberry or mini marshmallow, on the skewer before adding the other items.

It's usually best to slide food onto the pointed end of a skewer and poke the blunt end into the base, unless directed otherwise. If necessary, make starter holes in the base with a toothpick or skewer point.

Have Fun

Use the step-by-step directions in this book to make these stunning dessert bouquets. Then, be creative and make each bouquet unique by changing out colors and other design elements to make it your own.

Pretty in Pink

Chocolate-covered brownies with just enough pink detail to be spot-on!

You will need:

10 x 15″ jelly roll pan

1 (18.3 oz.) pkg. brownie mix*

Eggs, vegetable oil and water as directed on brownie mix package

Container (Sample uses a round cardboard canister, 5″ tall and 4½″ in diameter.)

Styrofoam

Pink shredded paper

2 thin rubber bands

2 to 3 (5 oz.) pkgs. Oreo Funstix

Wide decorative ribbon

Base (such as a 6″ cardboard circle or flat platter)

Flower-shaped cookie cutter (2½″ to 3″)

7 (8″) white lollipop sticks

1 (16 oz.) pkg. chocolate candy coating

½ C. pink candy wafers

Pastry bag fitted with small round tips

*One batch of brownies yields about 15 flower shapes, enough for 2 bouquets.

To Begin…

1 Preheat oven to 350°. Spray the jelly roll pan with nonstick cooking spray; set aside. In a large bowl, combine brownie mix, eggs, oil and water as directed on package. Spread batter in prepared pan and bake for 16 to 18 minutes or until a toothpick inserted 2″ from edge of pan comes out clean. Cool completely.

2 Wrap waxed paper around container and tape to hold in place; tuck excess over top edge of container. Cut Styrofoam to fit container, ending about 1″ below top edge. Wrap foam in aluminum foil, place in container and cover the top with shredded paper.

3 Stretch rubber bands around prepared container near the top and bottom. Carefully insert Oreo Funstix vertically under both rubber bands, one at a time, until container is covered and ends line up with bottom of container. Roll rubber bands toward the middle and tie ribbon around container as desired to hide rubber bands. For added stability, set container on the cardboard circle or platter.

4 Cut out brownie flowers with the cookie cutter, pressing down firmly for clean-cut edges. For easy removal, loosen each flower with a spatula while cutter is still in place and lift from pan; gently press brownie flower out of cutter. Make at least 7 flowers.

5 Gently insert a lollipop stick through the edge of each brownie flower just past its center.

6 Follow the package directions to melt chocolate candy coating in the microwave; stir until smooth. Set a brownie flower on a fork and spoon melted chocolate over the top and sides of flower and over about ¼″ of the stick until coated smoothly; shake gently, allowing excess chocolate to drip back into container. Set on a wire cooling rack over waxed paper; let dry for 30 minutes. Repeat to coat all brownie flowers.

7 When dry, spread a thin layer of melted chocolate over the back of each brownie flower; let dry. Re-melt chocolate as needed.

8 Melt pink candy wafers in the microwave according to the package directions; stir until smooth. Spoon warm mixture into a pastry bag fitted with a small round tip. On the front side of each brownie, pipe pink outlines to define "petals" as shown. To make small polka dots, change to a smaller round tip and make small dots on petals as desired. Let dry.

9 Plan placement of brownie flowers, using the photo as a guide. Make starter holes in the foam base with a toothpick before inserting sticks. Trim off 3″ from the stick of the front center flower; insert stick into foam base so flower rests low in container. Cut off 1″ from sticks for the next 2 flowers and insert into foam just in back and to the sides of front flower. Arrange remaining flowers, working from front to back and pushing sticks into foam as far as necessary for a balanced bouquet.

The *Whole Kit* & Caboodle

It all stacks up to sweet fun—Scotcheroos, Kit Kats and M&Ms.

You will need:

9 (10") wooden or
    bamboo skewers
9 large yellow gumballs
9" round pan
8" or 9" square pan
12 C. Special K cereal
3 C. peanut butter
2 C. light corn syrup
2 C. sugar

2 C. milk chocolate chips
2 C. butterscotch chips
Base (Sample uses a
    13" round glass platter,
    bottom side up.)
6 (3.92 oz.) pkgs. snack size
    Kit Kats (about 48)
1 (42 oz.) bag M&Ms
Wide rick-rack trim

To Begin...

1) Push the pointed end of 1 skewer into the center of each gumball; set aside. Line round and square pans (at least 1½" deep) with waxed paper; set aside. Pour cereal into a large bowl; set aside.

2) In a large saucepan over medium heat, combine peanut butter, corn syrup and sugar. Cook until sugar is dissolved, stirring occasionally. Pour mixture over cereal in bowl and stir until well combined. Spread cereal mixture evenly in prepared pans and press firmly.

3) Using the waxed paper, remove cereal mixture from the 9" round pan. Center the cereal disk upside down on the base to form the bottom layer. Peel off waxed paper and discard.

4 Using the waxed paper, remove the cereal mixture from the square pan. Place the cereal square upside down on a cutting board. Peel off waxed paper and discard. To make patterns, draw and cut out 1 (6″) and 1 (3″) circle on parchment paper. Fit patterns on top of the cereal square as shown in photo and use a sharp knife to cut around each circle to make 2 more round layers; set aside.

5 In a microwave-safe bowl, combine chocolate and butterscotch chips and melt in the microwave; stir until smooth. Spread an even layer of chocolate mixture over the top of the 9″ layer.

Center the 6″ layer on the first layer and frost the top of the second layer. Place the 3″ layer on top of that; frost the top and side of the third layer. Reserve remaining chocolate mixture for step 7.

6 Immediately place Kit Kats vertically* around the side of the top layer until covered, pressing to affix candy to the chocolate mixture. Cut Kit Kats to fit, if necessary.

7) Attach Kit Kats around the middle and bottom layers by placing a dab of reserved chocolate mixture on the bottom 1″ of the back side of candy and pressing to fasten securely*.

8) Pour M&Ms over each cereal layer, filling to the top of the Kit Kats.

9) Press the blunt end of each gumball skewer into the top layer, varying the heights as desired. Attach rick-rack trim around middle of bottom layer.

*Be sure to line up the Kit Kat bars so that the words, "Kit Kat", run the same direction on each layer.

Note

A single layer can be made instead of 3 layers simply by adjusting the amounts of ingredients, if desired.

Berried
Treasure
Tree

This stunning tree is
dressed to impress.

You will need:

Approximately 160 medium to large strawberries

Styrofoam cone (Sample is 17″ tall with a 4¾″ diameter base.)

1 sheet red tissue paper

Round toothpicks

Base (Sample uses an 8½″ round plate.)

8 to 10 sprigs fresh mint leaves

¼ C. white baking chips or bittersweet chocolate chips, optional

Small food-safe paintbrush, optional

Additional medium and large mint leaves, optional

Chocolate Sauce, optional (recipe follows)

To Begin...

1) Rinse strawberries in cool water and gently remove leaves (but do not cut berries) on all but one large berry (for top of cone); drain well and pat dry. Sort berries in groups of similar sizes, from largest to smallest.

2) Cut off 2″ from pointed top of Styrofoam cone. Wrap cone in aluminum foil. Cover foil with tissue paper, folding excess tissue over the top to make a flat surface; tape as needed.

3) Begin assembly around the bottom of cone with the largest strawberries. Push a toothpick horizontally into the cone, about ½″ from lower edge, so half of toothpick is exposed. Slide the stem end of 1 large strawberry onto toothpick until it touches cone (side of berry should be even with bottom of cone). Moving around the bottom of cone, insert another toothpick at the same height, about 1″ away, allowing enough space

for the next berry to fit. Slide a similar sized strawberry onto this toothpick (strawberries should touch). Fill in the bottom row with berries. In the same manner, place a second row of toothpicks and strawberries above first row, with strawberries just touching to hide most of the tissue paper.

4) Working in rows around the cone from the bottom toward the top, continue to insert toothpicks and strawberries, with largest berries toward the bottom and smaller ones toward the top. When cone is about half covered, transfer to the plate for easier handling. Continue to attach strawberries until cone is covered.

5) Insert a toothpick into the top of cone and slide the leaf end of the reserved strawberry onto toothpick.

6) To finish, insert mint sprigs between berries as desired.

Chocolate Leaves

To embellish your centerpiece with edible chocolate leaves, melt ¼ cup white baking chips or bittersweet chocolate chips in the microwave and stir until smooth. Set medium and large mint leaves on waxed paper. Dip the paintbrush into melted chocolate and brush generously over leaves; let dry to the touch. Coat leaves with a second layer of melted chocolate and let dry for 30 minutes. Carefully peel off mint leaves and discard. Arrange chocolate leaves among strawberries as desired.

Chocolate Sauce

Serve warm chocolate sauce alongside the fresh berries, if desired. Place 2 cups semi-sweet or bittersweet chocolate chips in a large bowl; set aside. In a medium saucepan over low heat, combine 1 cup heavy whipping cream, ⅓ cup sugar and ⅓ cup light corn syrup. Bring mixture to a boil, stirring frequently. Remove from heat and pour over chocolate chips in bowl; let stand until chocolate melts. Stir until smooth. Stir in 1½ teaspoons vanilla extract and serve.

Pie to Go

Sweet little fruit pies tucked
into an eat-on-the-go bouquet.

You will need:

Styrofoam

Container (Sample uses a ceramic pot, 5½″ tall and 3¾″ in diameter.)

Shredded tissue paper

1 (14.1 oz.) pkg. ready-to-use pie crust (2 crusts)

Round cookie cutters (2″ to 2½″)

12 white lollipop and/or cookie sticks (4″, 6″, 7″ or 8″)

Fruit pie filling or preserves of choice (Sample uses blueberry and strawberry pie filling and apricot preserves.)

Milk, divided

Sugar

¾ C. powdered sugar

Pastry bag fitted with a small round tip

Zippered plastic bags, optional

Narrow ribbon to match filling colors

To Begin...

1) Line a large baking sheet with parchment paper. Preheat oven to 400°. Cut Styrofoam to fit into container, leaving 1″ of space at the top. Wrap foam in aluminum foil and press into container. Cover top with shredded tissue paper.

2) Let pie crusts stand at room temperature for 15 minutes. Handling 1 crust at a time, gently unroll on a flat surface. With cookie cutters, cut out matching pairs of circles, cutting as many as will fit.

3) Place pairs of crust circles on prepared pan. Press 1 lollipop or cookie stick on 1 circle of each pair, about ¾ of the way across circle. Use different lengths of sticks, placing the shortest and longest sticks on the smallest pies. Place about a teaspoonful of filling or preserves in the center, covering the end of stick and leaving about ³⁄₈″ uncovered around outside edge.

4) With a fingertip dipped in water, dampen the outside edge of pastry circle. Place the matching circle on top and press edges together with a fingertip. With fingers, press crust against stick.

Press the end of a short lollipop stick around the edge of crust to seal and create an indented pattern.

5) Brush the top of pies with milk and sprinkle with sugar.

6) Bake for 15 to 17 minutes or until golden brown; remove from oven. Carefully remove any filling that has seeped from the pies. Cool pies completely. Use fresh parchment paper to bake each batch of pies.

7) Whisk together powdered sugar with enough milk to make a thick smooth icing. Place icing into the pastry bag fitted with a small round tip and pipe lines across as many pies as desired. Let stand at least 15 minutes.

8) Cut a 12″ piece of ribbon for each pie. (Match ribbon color to filling, if desired.) Tie a small snug bow around stick under each pie.

9) To arrange, press sticks into base, starting with largest pies in the center and alternating colors as desired. Fill in front and back with smaller pies using photo as a guide.

Party Favors

For easy transport, insert each pie into a zippered plastic bag; fold corners to the back and tie a ribbon around the stick, gathering plastic. Trim off the zippered edge of bag with sharp scissors.

For Your
Sweet Side

Ho Ho swirls and fresh fruit make a quick and yummy bouquet.

You will need:

1 whole fresh pineapple

8 Ho Ho chocolate cake rolls

20 fresh medium
    strawberries

2 bananas (ripe but firm)

2 T. lemon juice

16 to 20 (10″) wooden or
    bamboo skewers

1 (10 oz.) pkg. frozen
    sweetened
    strawberries, thawed,
    optional

To Begin...

1) Prepare a pineapple "boat" for the base. Set the pineapple upright (leaves up). With a sharp knife, cut through pineapple from top to bottom, in front of the leaves and core, to remove about ⅓ of pineapple. Reserve the large section with leaves; slice remaining section lengthwise into 3 even wedges. Slice each wedge crosswise (through the flesh only) in 1″ intervals; cut off the skin to separate the chunks of pineapple. Set pineapple chunks aside and discard skin.

2) Slice each cake roll crosswise into 3 equal pieces; set aside.

3 Cut off the stem end just below the leafy cap of each strawberry; set aside fruit and discard leaves.

4 Peel bananas and cut crosswise into slices about 1″ wide. Gently coat banana slices in lemon juice to prevent browning. Drain on paper towels and set aside.

5 Alternately and in any combination, thread pieces of fruit and cake roll onto pointed end of skewers to make the following: 1 skewer with 2 pieces; 6 skewers with 3 pieces; 3 skewers with 4 pieces; 3 skewers with 5 pieces and 3 skewers with 6 pieces. Slide pieces toward the pointed end of each skewer, leaving about 2″ of pointed end exposed for pushing skewers into the pineapple base.

6 If necessary, trim off a slice of skin from bottom side of pineapple base so it rests flat. To assemble bouquet, push pointed end of skewers down into the cut side of base until food touches the pineapple and skewers are secure. Insert the smallest skewer first, placing it near the rounded edge near leaves. With the pruning shears, trim off the blunt end of this skewer so about 1″ remains exposed.

7) Build the bouquet diagonally across the pineapple by inserting 2 rows of 3-piece skewers behind the smallest skewer; trim off blunt end of each skewer to 1". Continue to insert skewers of increasing length while working toward the back of the bouquet. Trim blunt ends as needed. The tallest skewers should be placed at the back of bouquet. If necessary, make starter holes in the tough core area of the pineapple with another skewer.

8) Serve bouquet with small bowls of strawberry sauce for dipping, if desired. To make strawberry sauce, place thawed strawberries in a blender container and blend until smooth.

Candied
Pansies

Candy corn tops crispy
treats to create pretty flowers,
sweet enough to eat!

You will need:

8″ square baking dish
3 T. butter
30 standard marshmallows
3¾ C. crisp rice cereal
18 (7″ to 8″) white
 cookie sticks
About 5 squares white
 almond bark, divided
1 (14 oz.) pkg. pastel
 candy corn

18 yellow or brown
 M&Ms
Container (Sample uses
 a 4″ square ceramic
 pot, 3½″ deep.)
4″ Styrofoam ball
Green tissue paper
Green curling ribbon

To Begin...

1) Spray the baking dish with nonstick cooking spray; set aside. In a large saucepan over medium-low heat, melt butter. Add marshmallows, stirring constantly until melted and smooth. Remove from heat. Stir in cereal until well coated. Press mixture evenly in prepared dish. Cool 15 minutes; chill in refrigerator for 20 minutes.

2) With a sharp knife, trim off and remove about ¼″ around edge of pan. Cut cereal treats into 1⅛″ to 1¼″ square pieces. Remove from pan and press a cookie stick into the center of each square. Place in freezer to chill.

3) Meanwhile, follow the package directions to melt 2 squares almond bark in the microwave; stir until smooth. Holding the stick of 1 cereal square over the melted bark, spoon bark over square until coated, letting excess drip back into

container. Set on waxed paper to dry. Repeat to coat about half the squares. Melt 2 more squares of almond bark to coat remaining cereal squares.

4) With a toothpick, mark the center top of each coated square. Gather 7 like-colored candies for each flower.

5) Melt the remaining square of almond bark as directed. With a spoon, spread a small amount of bark over half of the top of a coated square, avoiding toothpick hole in the center. Quickly set several pieces of candy corn into wet bark, placing points near the toothpick hole and colored parts radiating out from the center like flower petals. Hold for several seconds until set. Repeat process to attach remaining candy corn so flower has 7 candies with a space in the middle.

6) Place a drop of melted bark in the center between petal tips and quickly set 1 M&M in place; hold until set.

7) Push cookie stick into waxed paper-covered Styrofoam to dry. Repeat steps 5-7 to complete about 18 flowers.

8) Wrap Styrofoam ball in aluminum foil and cover with green tissue paper. Set into container.

9) To arrange bouquet, press cookie sticks into foam, starting at the center top of ball for tallest flowers. Trim sticks as necessary, placing shortest flowers around the edges to fill in bouquet so it looks nice from all directions.

10) Curl 8″ pieces of ribbon and wrap them around the sticks near base. Cut 5″ squares of tissue paper, pinch the centers and gather to make tufts; tuck tufts into bouquet as desired to cover base and sticks.

Truffle Tower

Delight a chocolate lover with a tower of tasty truffles.

You will need:

- Styrofoam cone (Sample is 12″ tall with a 3¾″ diameter base.)
- Brown craft paper
- 3 (12 oz.) pkgs. semi-sweet chocolate chips, divided
- 2¼ C. sweetened condensed milk, divided
- ½ tsp. orange extract
- ½ tsp. raspberry flavoring
- ½ tsp. almond extract
- 1 C. sliced almonds, finely ground
- 7 squares white almond bark, divided
- Styrofoam sheet covered with waxed paper
- 7 squares chocolate-flavored almond bark, divided
- Round toothpicks
- Zippered plastic bags
- Red foil or cellophane
- Base (Sample uses an 8½″ plate.)
- Wide decorative ribbon

To Begin...

1) Wrap Styrofoam cone in aluminum foil. Cover foil with brown paper, folding it over the top and trimming off excess paper; tape as needed and set aside.

2) Melt 1 package chocolate chips in the microwave, stirring until smooth. Stir in ¾ cup sweetened condensed milk until well mixed. Blend in orange extract. Cover bowl and chill for 45 minutes.

3) In a clean bowl, melt another package chocolate chips and stir in ¾ cup sweetened condensed milk until blended. Stir in raspberry flavoring. Cover and chill for 45 minutes.

4 In the same manner, melt the last package of chocolate chips and stir in remaining ¾ cup sweetened condensed milk. Add almond extract and stir well.

Do not chill, but instead, use the small end of a melon baller to scoop out a ball of dough. With hands, roll dough into a smooth 1″ ball. Roll ball in ground almonds until coated; set on a baking sheet. Repeat with remaining dough; cover and chill until assembly.

5 Shape orange-flavored dough into smooth 1″ balls as directed in step 4; place on a baking sheet and refrigerate. Repeat to make 1″ balls from raspberry-flavored dough. Place on a baking sheet and chill.

6 Follow the package directions to melt 6 squares white almond bark in the microwave; stir until smooth. Pour melted bark into a deep mug. Working with a few orange-flavored truffle balls at a time (leave remaining truffles in the refrigerator), insert a toothpick about halfway into each ball. Dip each ball into melted white bark to coat; let excess drip back into mug. Stand each truffle upright to dry by inserting the end of its toothpick into waxed paper-covered Styrofoam. Repeat to coat all orange-flavored truffles with white bark.

7 In the same way, melt 6 squares chocolate-flavored bark in the microwave; stir until smooth. Pour melted bark into a deep mug. Working with small batches, insert a toothpick about halfway into each raspberry-flavored truffle ball. Dip balls into melted chocolate bark to coat; let excess drip back into mug. Push toothpicks into waxed paper-covered foam to dry. Repeat to coat all raspberry-flavored truffles with chocolate bark.

8) Melt remaining square white bark in the microwave, stirring until smooth. Pour warm mixture into a zippered plastic bag. Cut off a tiny corner of bag and drizzle white bark back and forth over chocolate truffles. Let dry. In the same manner, melt remaining square of chocolate bark in the microwave, stirring until smooth. Pour into another plastic bag, cut off corner and drizzle over white truffles. Let dry.

9) Wrap 10 to 12 truffles in red foil or cellophane, using tape to secure as needed.

10) Starting near the base of the cone, make a horizontal starter hole by inserting a toothpick deeply into cone and removing. Insert 1 truffle on its toothpick into starter hole. About 1″ to the side of first hole, make another starter hole; insert a second truffle, edges touching. Continue working in rows around cone, alternating flavors and several red truffles, until cone is half covered; transfer to the plate. Continue inserting truffles to cover cone. Lay center of ribbon across top of cone; insert a red truffle and its toothpick through ribbon and into foam.

Orange Dips

A beautiful burst of sweet citrus dipped in creamy chocolate.

You will need:

5 fresh oranges

1½ C. chocolate candy wafers, divided

30 (10″) wooden or bamboo skewers

Styrofoam sheet covered with waxed paper

Zippered plastic bag

1 head iceburg lettuce

Container (Sample uses a flower pot, 4½″ tall and 4″ in diameter.)

Green kale

To Begin...

1 Cut each orange in half from the top to the bottom. Cut each half into 3 even wedges. Place cut side of orange wedges on paper towels to remove excess juice from the surface. Turn wedges over to remove excess juice from the other cut surface.

2 Melt about ½ cup of candy wafers in the microwave according to the package directions; stir until smooth.

3 Poke the pointed end of a skewer through the center of the peel of one orange wedge. Holding onto skewer, dip both cut sides of orange into melted chocolate, covering the flesh of the orange as well as about ¼″ to ⅜″ of the orange peel on each side of the wedge.

Poke blunt end of skewer into Styrofoam. Repeat with 15 more orange wedges, melting more candy wafers, ½ cup at a time, as needed. Let set until chocolate is dry.

4) Pour about ½ cup of remaining melted chocolate into a zippered plastic bag. Cut off a tiny piece from one corner of bag and drizzle melted chocolate designs over flesh of 10 orange wedges as desired. Let chocolate dry. Dip or decorate remaining wedges if needed.

5) Remove skewers from dried dipped oranges and cut skewers to 5″. Reinsert the pointed end of skewer into narrow end of an orange wedge, about ½″ from tip. Repeat with all dipped oranges. Cut 10 skewers to 5″ and insert skewers in the same manner into a narrow end of each drizzled orange wedge.

6) Remove a few leaves from the head of lettuce as needed to fit snugly into the container. Place lettuce head in container so the top of lettuce mounds about 1″ above the rim. Push some of the remaining leaves into the container around lettuce head to hold it snugly in place, if needed. Cover top of lettuce with kale. (The skewers will hold the kale in place.)

7) Beginning along the edge of container, insert the blunt end of 12 dipped skewers into lettuce head so orange wedges set at about a 45° angle, with the chocolate side facing down and the narrow end of the orange wedge on the outside of container.

8) For the next row, insert skewers with drizzled orange wedges into lettuce head so the orange peel rests partially on the first row of orange wedges, decorated side facing up.

9) Insert skewers with the 4 remaining dipped oranges nearly vertically in the center of lettuce head so the narrow ends of orange wedges touch in the center.

10) Tuck additional kale around the outer edge of container as desired.

Autumn Splendor

Pumpkin-flavored cookies
match the all-around festive
tone of this bouquet.

You will need:

2 C. prepared white decorator icing, divided

Gel or paste food coloring (yellow, gold, orange, brown, red)

Pastry bag fitted with medium round and leaf tips

Yellow nonpareils

Pumpkin Sugar Cookie Dough (recipe on page 60)

Cookie cutters (1½″ round, several 3″ to 4″ leaves, 2½″ acorn)

Drinking straw, optional*

Cookie Icing (recipe on page 60)

1 to 2 squares white almond bark

Small pumpkin (Sample is 7″ tall and 6½″ in diameter.)

Candle (Sample is a brown pillar candle, 3″ tall and 3″ in diameter.)

Base (Sample is a branch wreath, 18″ in diameter with a 5″ opening.)

To Begin...

1) Tint ½ cup decorator icing bright yellow with food coloring. Tint remaining 1½ cups decorator icing bright orange.

2) Place yellow icing into the pastry bag fitted with the round tip. Cut waxed paper into 20 (1½″) squares. To pipe the yellow center of each flower, squeeze icing from the bag onto the middle of a waxed paper square until the center of the flower is ⅜″ to ½″ high. Pick

up the waxed paper square and immediately dip the yellow center into nonpareils.

Place orange icing into another pastry bag fitted with the leaf tip. To pipe the orange petals, squeeze icing from bag, lifting as pressure is released from bag and "laying" the icing petals from the yellow center toward

the outside. Continue around the center as shown, petals touching. In the same manner, pipe 2 shorter rows on top of the first row, beginning at yellow center and staggering each row so the petals fall between those in the previous row. Set aside. Repeat to make 20 flowers. Cover loosely and let stand overnight or for up to 5 days.

3. Prepare Pumpkin Sugar Cookie Dough using the recipe on page 60. Roll out chilled dough to a thickness of ¼″ to ⅜″. Cut out about 10 large leaves, 10 medium leaves, 6 to 8 small leaves, 10 acorns and 30 small rounds. (Cut hanging holes before baking if desired*.) Bake cookies at 375° for 9 to 13 minutes or until lightly browned on bottom. Cool completely on a wire rack. Serve any extra cookies alongside the bouquet or save for another use.

4. Prepare Cookie Icing using the recipe on page 60 or use additional decorator icing. Divide icing between 4 bowls. To each bowl, add food coloring to create desired shades of red, orange, yellow and brown. Frost leaves as desired, dragging knife to make a leaf-like texture on top. Frost acorns brown. Let icing dry at least 2 hours.

5. Follow the package directions to melt 1 square almond bark in the microwave, stirring until smooth. Using a metal offset spatula, carefully remove an icing flower from waxed paper square and attach it to a small round cookie with a dab of melted bark, pressing gently on the yellow center. Decorate 20 round cookies with icing flowers. Let dry. Reserve remaining bark.

6 Break off pumpkin stem. Set candle on top of pumpkin and trace around it with a pencil. With a sharp knife, cut along traced line and remove top. Scoop out seeds. Set candle into carved hole to check fit; trim opening as needed for easy removal of candle. Set aside. Crumple aluminum foil to fill pumpkin; set candle into hole on top of foil and adjust height.

7 To assemble, cover top of wreath with plastic wrap. Set pumpkin in center opening of wreath. Arrange leaf, acorn and plain round cookies around pumpkin on plastic, alternating shapes and colors. Arrange 9 or 10 flower cookies on top of leaf cookies.

8 Re-melt reserved almond bark in the microwave; stir until smooth. Attach flower cookies around pumpkin opening by placing a dab of melted bark on the back of a cookie and pressing it against pumpkin until set. Repeat to make a row of about 10 flowers.

To hang cookies from pumpkin, use a straw to poke a hole in cookies before baking. After baking, cooling and frosting, thread ribbon or jute through hole, tie a knot and attach to cut edge of pumpkin with a toothpick.

Sunny-Side Up

Shed a little sunshine
with this cookie and
cupcake bouquet.

You will need:

Muffin pan

Paper cupcake liners

1 (18.2 oz.) pkg. yellow cake mix

Eggs, vegetable oil and water as directed on cake mix package

Styrofoam (Sample uses a disk, 1″ thick and 5³/₄″ in diameter and a ball, 6″ in diameter.)

Container (Sample uses a metal bucket, 5¹/₂″ deep and 7″ in diameter.)

Filler (Sample uses brown shredded paper.)

18 wooden or bamboo skewers

18 (2 oz.) plastic cups*

9 Oreo cookies (or more as needed)

2 C. prepared white decorator icing

Gel or paste food coloring (yellow)

Pastry bag fitted with a medium star tip

To Begin...

1 Preheat oven to 350°. Line muffin cups with paper liners; set aside. Prepare cake batter as directed on cake mix package. Fill liners about ¹/₂ full with batter. Bake as directed on package; set aside to cool completely.

2 Place Styrofoam disk in bucket, firmly pressing down until level and securely lodged in bucket. Cut a thin slice from one side of foam ball and place flat side on foam disk in bucket. Fill gap between foam ball and bucket with filler. Place some filler over foam ball.

3 Trim skewers to 3½″ to 4″ lengths. Poke pointed end of skewer through the bottom center of a plastic cup. Insert blunt end of skewer into foam ball, positioning so the side edge of cup rests on top edge of bucket. Push skewer deeply into foam until the bottom of the cup rests against the foam ball and the pointed end of the skewer protrudes about 1″ through the center of cup. Continue around perimeter of bucket and then work upward until foam ball is covered with skewers and plastic cups.

4 Separate the 2 halves of each cookie, removing the cream centers. Tint icing with yellow food coloring as desired. Frost cupcakes with a thin layer of icing. Carefully place a cupcake in each plastic cup, pushing it onto skewer. Immediately press 1 cookie half in the center of each frosted cupcake.

5 Place remaining icing into the pastry bag. Pipe a row of short icing petals around each cookie by squeezing the bag, then lifting and "laying" the icing out and upward, ending the petal halfway between the edge of cookie and the edge of cupcake. Make a second row of petals, starting at the outer edge of previous petals and ending at edge of cupcake, positioning petals between previous petals. Tuck extra filler between cupcakes as desired.

*Or cut 18 (8 oz.) Styrofoam cups to 1″ or 1½″ in height.

Garden
Roundup

*Fresh fruits star in this
flower garden.*

You will need:

- Melon baller
- ½ cantaloupe
- 1 whole fresh pineapple
- Cookie cutters (2″ and 3¼″ flowers, 2½″ butterfly, 1⅝″ star, 1″ round)
- 2 large oranges
- 1 large red apple
- Lemon juice
- 3 kiwifruit
- 2 green apples
- 1 bunch red seedless grapes (50 to 60)
- 1 pt. strawberries (about 25)
- 2 heads iceberg lettuce
- Container (Sample uses a 5½″ x 10″ oblong basket, 3″ deep.)
- 1 yellow apple, optional
- Fresh parsley
- 50 to 60 (10″ and 12″) wooden or bamboo skewers
- ½ C. white baking chips, optional
- 1 square chocolate-flavored almond bark, optional
- Small plastic bag, optional

To Begin...

1) Use the melon baller to cut small and large balls from the cantaloupe; set on a rimmed baking sheet.

2) Cut the pineapple crosswise to make 5 (¾″- thick) disks. Center the large flower cookie cutter over 1 pineapple disk. (Metal cookie cutters are recommended for a clean, even cut.) Press straight down on the cookie cutter, using even pressure. Gently slide the flower shape out of the disk. Repeat to make 2 more flowers. Reserve skins. With the 1″ round cookie cutter, cut out the center core of each pineapple flower; discard core. Insert a large melon ball into the hole in each pineapple flower. (Fit should be snug).

3 From the 2 remaining pineapple disks, use cookie cutters to cut out 3 small flowers and 1 butterfly.

4 Cut out small wedges from reserved pineapple skins and any remaining pineapple, cutting through both the skin and flesh. Set all pineapple shapes on the rimmed baking sheet and refrigerate.

5 Cut oranges crosswise into ½″-thick slices. Gently peel off and discard rind; refrigerate orange slices.

6 Cut red apple into 4 crosswise slices, about ⅜″ thick. Use the star cookie cutter to cut out the center of each apple slice; discard center. Dip apple slices in lemon juice to prevent browning; set aside.

7 Cut kiwifruit into ⅜″-thick slices, making as many as possible. Press the star cookie cutter into the center of the largest slices to cut out 4 kiwi stars. Insert a kiwi star into each red apple slice.

8 Cut green apples into ³/₈″-thick slices. Use the center slices with the best star detail. With one point of the small star-shaped cookie cutter, cut out evenly spaced notches around the edge of each slice; carefully remove any seeds. Dip slices in lemon juice.

9 Insert a skewer up through the center bottom of each small pineapple flower, with point sticking out the top; attach a grape to each point. Add a raisin or other dried fruit "stopper" below the fruit to hold flower in place.

10 Push the point of several skewers through 2 to 6 grapes, strawberries and cantaloupe balls without piercing the top fruit. Combine fruits as desired, making both long and short skewers.

Carefully insert a 10″ skewer halfway through each slice of kiwi, red and green apple and orange until secure. Insert 12″ skewers into the edge of each large pineapple flower and butterfly, about ³/₄ of the way across flower.

11 Begin assembly by placing the largest pineapple flowers, apples and oranges first, trimming skewers as necessary. Fill in around these large pieces with remaining skewers of fruit, placing tallest pieces in back and trimming skewers as needed.

Chocolate-Covered Strawberries

To add flavor and elegance, melt ½ cup white baking chips in the microwave and stir until smooth. With strawberries on skewers, dip berries in melted white coating until covered, allowing excess to drip off; set upright in Styrofoam to dry. Melt 1 square chocolate-flavored almond bark and pour warm mixture into a zippered plastic bag. Cut a tiny piece off one corner of bag and pipe fine lines of chocolate over berries; let dry. Insert coated berries in bouquet as desired.

Minty
Blooms

*Eating a tree
never tasted so good!*

You will need:

- 3 squares chocolate-flavored almond bark
- 5 to 6 (10 oz.) pkgs. chocolate-covered cookies (such as Keebler Grasshopper cookies)
- Round toothpicks
- 6 large sheets green tissue paper (or another color)
- Decorative scissors
- Styrofoam cone (Sample is 17″ tall with a 4¾″ diameter base.)
- Base (Sample uses a ceramic pedestal, 4″ tall and 6″ in diameter.)

To Begin...

1) Melt almond bark in the microwave according to the package directions; stir until smooth.

2) Line up a few cookies on a flat work surface, bottom side up. Spoon a small amount of melted bark on the center of each cookie and press a toothpick into melted bark, about halfway across cookie. Quickly set a second cookie on top of toothpick and bark, edges even, to make sandwich cookies; toothpick should stick out about 1½″. Hold in place several seconds until set. Repeat to make approximately 100 sandwich cookies. Set aside and let dry completely.

3. Make a pattern by cutting out a 4½″ square piece of paper. On a sheet of tissue paper, trace around the pattern as many times as possible. Stack sheets of tissue paper together and use decorative scissors to cut through the layers as traced. (You will need about 100 squares.)

4. Fold each tissue paper square as shown on the pattern to make a "pleated pocket." To do this, first fold the square along diagonal dotted line to within ¾″ of the opposite sides. With the fold at the bottom, bring the lower left and right corners toward the center until folded edges meet in the middle and sides are lined up. Crease well to create a square pocket with opening at the top.

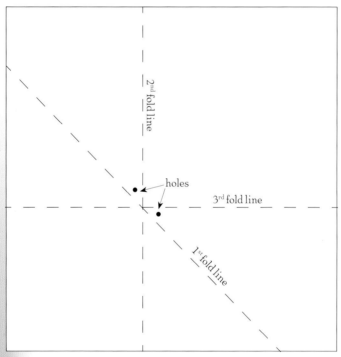

2nd fold line

holes

3rd fold line

1st fold line

Pleated Pocket Pattern

Enlarge square to 4½″ and cut 100 squares from tissue paper.

5) With a plain toothpick, make 2 starter holes through the folded tip in each pocket as shown on pattern. Remove toothpick. Insert sandwich cookie, pushing the point of its toothpick through both starter holes so cookie is inside the pocket.

6) Cut off 2″ from top of Styrofoam cone. Wrap cone in aluminum foil. Cover foil with tissue paper, twisting the excess tissue paper at the top into a tuft.

7) To assemble, press the toothpick of each cookie and pocket horizontally into the foam to make a row around the bottom of cone, placing cookies close together. Place pleated side of each pocket facing up. Insert another row above first row, staggering cookies between previous ones. Continue to insert rows of cookie pockets, working from bottom to top until cone is covered. Remove final cookie from its tissue pocket; insert toothpick and cookie into the tissue tuft on top of cone. Arrange the tissue pocket behind cookie in tuft as desired. Carefully lift cone and set it on pedestal before serving.

Hot Cocoa Stir Sticks

Stir some fun and flavor into a mug of hot cocoa with these chocolate-dipped marshmallows on a stick. Change up the flavors with different candy toppers.

4 (5″ to 6″) plastic drink stirrers
4 standard marshmallows
Chopped or crushed candies*
3 T. chocolate chips (dark, semi-sweet or milk chocolate)
Styrofoam
3 packets hot cocoa mix
Mini marshmallows

1) For each stir stick, push a plastic drink stirrer into one end of a standard marshmallow, without piercing the other end; set aside.

2) Set the chopped or crushed candy on a flat work surface.

3) In a microwave-safe bowl, melt chocolate chips in the microwave; stir until smooth. Dip the top half of each marshmallow into the chocolate, shaking gently to let excess chocolate drip back into bowl. Immediately dip the top into the chopped or crushed candies to coat. Press end of plastic stirrer into Styrofoam and let dry, about 1 hour.

4) Cut a small piece of foam about 2″ tall and about 1″ smaller than diameter of mug; cover with aluminum foil and insert into mug. Tuck cocoa packets between foam and mug. Press ends of stirrers into foam, staggering heights. Fill mug with mini marshmallows.

*Try Hershey's Hugs, Andes mints, Reese's peanut butter cups or peppermint sticks. You will need to crush or chop about 2 pieces of candy (or 1 peppermint stick) to cover 4 marshmallows.

Cake Ball Place Markers

Decorate your table with a tiny dessert that doubles as a place marker.

Prepared 9 x 13″ cake, any flavor

1 (16 oz.) tub frosting, any flavor

4″ white lollipop sticks

2 to 3 squares chocolate candy coating

2 to 3 squares white almond bark

Pastry bag fitted with small round tip

Narrow decorative ribbon

1) Cut away and discard ¼″ around edges of cake. Finely crumble remaining cake into a large bowl and stir in frosting; blend well.

2) Roll mixture into 1¼″ balls; set on waxed paper-lined baking sheets. Insert a lollipop stick into the center of each ball. Freeze 1 hour.

3) Remove 10 balls from freezer (leave remainder frozen until needed.) Follow package directions to melt candy coating in the microwave; stir until smooth. Dip balls into melted chocolate and lightly shake to remove excess. Set upright on waxed paper to dry. Repeat to coat half the cake balls. Melt almond bark and coat remaining cake balls. Let set until dry.

4) Reheat remaining almond bark and pour into the pastry bag. Decorate the chocolate-dipped balls with piped-on initials or other designs. Reheat remaining chocolate coating and decorate the white balls in the same way. Tie ribbon around each stick.

Sweet Endings

Perked-Up Peppermints

Turn thick 4" peppermint sticks into party-perfect after-dinner desserts when you coat them in chocolate and pistachios.

¼ C. shelled pistachio nuts, pecans or almonds
¼ C. bittersweet chocolate chips
¼ tsp. solid shortening
10 (4") peppermint sticks
Container (Sample uses a glass dessert dish, 3½" in diameter.)
White sugar
Red sugar

1 On a cutting board, finely chop nuts; set aside.

2 In a microwave-safe bowl, melt chocolate chips in microwave; stir until smooth. Stir in shortening until melted.

3 Spoon chocolate over one end of a peppermint stick until half of stick is coated in chocolate. Promptly roll in chopped nuts and set on waxed paper to dry. Repeat to coat 9 additional peppermint sticks in chocolate and nuts.

4 To display and serve, fill dessert dish halfway with white sugar. Pour a layer of red sugar over the top, using a funnel as needed to direct the sugar around the edges of dish. Carefully spoon another layer of white sugar on top. Insert the end of each peppermint stick into the sugar.

For Fun Gift-Giving

Stack 3 peppermint sticks together and tie a ribbon around the center. Wrap in cellophane.

Flower Pot Cookies

This quick and easy bouquet made with purchased butter cookies and gumdrops adds a touch of sweet color to any table. Choose colors to fit your party theme.

2 squares white almond bark

8 flower-shaped butter cookies with a hole in the center

8 gumdrops

Nonpareils

Decorating sugar

8 wooden or bamboo skewers, cut to 4″ to 6″ lengths

Styrofoam

Container (Sample uses a flower pot, 3½″ tall and 3½″ in diameter.)

1 paper cupcake liner, flattened

1) Melt almond bark in the microwave according to package directions; stir until smooth. For each flower, cover the bottom side of a cookie with melted bark and press the flat side of a gumdrop on the wet bark, centered over the hole. Immediately sprinkle with nonpareils or decorating sugar. Set aside to dry.

2) Poke the pointed end of a skewer up through the hole in the cookie and about halfway through the gumdrop. Repeat with each skewer and cookie; set aside.

3) Cut Styrofoam to fit container, nearly even with the top edge. Wrap foam in aluminum foil and place in container. Cover foam with the flattened cupcake liner.

4) Insert blunt end of flower skewers into foam, alternating the height of flowers.

Recipes

Pumpkin Sugar Cookies

(Makes about 36)

³/₄ C. butter, softened

1 C. sugar

¹/₂ C. pumpkin puree

¹/₂ tsp. vanilla extract

2¹/₂ tsp. pumpkin pie spice

3 C. flour

1 tsp. baking powder

¹/₂ tsp. salt

In a large mixing bowl, beat butter on medium speed until creamy. Add sugar and beat until light and fluffy. Add pumpkin, vanilla and pie spice, beating until well blended. In a separate bowl, stir together flour, baking powder and salt. Add flour mixture to pumpkin mixture and beat until well mixed and a stiff dough forms. Cover and chill for at least 1 hour. Then follow cutting and baking directions on page 42 to make Autumn Splendor.

Cookie Icing

1¹/₂ T. meringue powder

2 C. powdered sugar

1 tsp. clear vanilla extract

¹/₂ tsp. butter flavoring

3 T. warm water

Low-fat milk

Gel or paste food coloring
(autumn colors)

In a medium mixing bowl, combine meringue powder, powdered sugar, vanilla, butter flavoring and water; beat on medium speed until smooth and fluffy, about 4 minutes. Stir in 1 to 2¹/₂ tablespoons milk, a little at a time, to reach desired spreading consistency. Then follow the directions on page 42 to tint and frost the pumpkin cookies used in Autumn Splendor.